Lots of Cats

Written by Michèle Dufresne

PIONEER VALLEY EDUCATIONAL PRESS, INC.

Look at the cat.
The cat can nap.

Cats like to sleep.
They sleep a lot.

Look at the cat.
The cat can nab the rat.

Cats like to hunt.
They like to hunt
birds and mice.

Look at the cat.
The cat is a **tiger**.
The tiger has **stripes**.

A tiger's stripes can be black or brown. The stripes on a tiger help it blend in with trees and grass.

Look at the cat.

The cat is tan.

The cat is a **lion**.

The male lion has a mane on its neck. Lions live in groups called prides.

Look at the cat.

The cat is a **bobcat**.

Do not pat a bobcat!

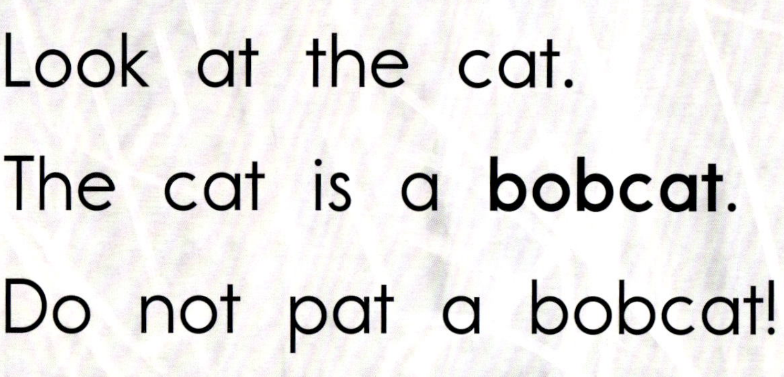

Bobcats are medium-sized wildcats. They have black bars on their forelegs and black-tipped stubby tails.

glossary